So, I've Been Thinking

Seemingly Random Thoughts on Leadership

Other Books By Karl Bimshas

"Leaders Don't Shrug"

"GO GET IT!"

"Pushing Back the Ocean"

"How to Stay When You Want to Quit"

"Disposable Journal"

"Write Advice"

"Perspectives"

So, I've Been Thinking

Seemingly Random Thoughts on Leadership

Karl Bimshas

BimMedia

San Diego, California

Copyright © 2013 by Karl Bimshas

All rights reserved. This publication or any portion thereof may not be reproduced, or used in and manner whatsoever without the express written permission of the publisher except for the use of brief quotations in a book review or scholarly journal.

First Printing: 2013

Karl Bimshas Consulting
7676 Hazard Center Drive, Suite 500
San Diego, CA 92108

www.KarlBimshasConsulting.com

ISBN   9781728847054

Dedication

For Mom and Dad, they continue to shape my views on leadership, creativity, America and countless other subjects in ways my words cannot adequately express, but I keep trying..

Table of Contents

Introduction 9
Bring Your Artist to Work 11
Solve the Damn Problem 15
How Did You Get To Be So Awesome? 19
Angry People Are Boring 21
It's Obvious 25
Autonomy, Responsibility, Scapegoating 29
Pelican Teamwork 33
61 Positive Actions To Consider 35
Nobody Wants to Wait 10 Years for Your Story 49
Wisdom from the Father and Son 51
Who Do You Wish More People Could Meet? 53
It's Your Fault. There, I Feel Better. 57
Write Anyway 59
My Leadership Point of View 61
Stop Wasting Your Talent 67
How I Became a Recovering Quitter 69
Be A Leader Even When You Don't Feel Like It 71
How to Keep Yourself From Burning Out 73
Let's Eradicate Despondency 77
Where are the Poets? 83
Valuing Liberty 85
Is Voting a Right, Privilege or Responsibility? 89
Thoughts on Cheering Freedom 93
A Parent America 97
they and me can again be We 101
Never Be Frozen By Fear 103
For the Love of Boston 107
Six Words of Advice for Writers 113
About the Author 117

Introduction

So, I've Been Thinking is a random collection of essays and anecdotes that capture a few of my thoughts on leadership, creativity, and America. I recognize that's a wide and varied scope, but I discovered a common denominator – the pursuit of excellence.

Many of the thoughts included in this volume were first expressed in my Reflections on Leadership newsletter or on one of my blogs. I've included the first published date, under a few titles in the hopes of building context to the piece. With luck, the majority of them stand alone with a timeless principle.

Please enjoy this sample of my writing. I'd love to know what you think. To join my mailing list or inquire about my consulting work, please visit www.KarlBimshasConsulting.com

-Karl Bimshas

Bring Your Artist to Work

September 30, 2010

Every child is an artist. The problem is how to remain an artist once we grow up.
-Pablo Picasso

The problem many people have with their work-life is that it serves more as a marker of time between weekends, holidays, vacations and milestones like a new car, home or college tuition instead of as a place of productivity and enrichment. As a result, some don't bring their best selves to the endeavor. Careers and industries have been built around the focus of solving this problem. Sadly, many of the solutions are short-lived, if adopted at all.

Here's an alternative to consider. Bring your artist to work.

Businesses are built on facts, figures, empirical data and market research. Important decisions are based on favorable ratios and return on investments. These are crucial, and it's shocking how many organizations, large and small, do not employ them. However, they are only part of the equation. They represent the head. Organizations need more heart, and that's what you need to use every day. When you bring your artist to work, you bring the best of your talents and abilities. You focus on your strengths and use them to accomplish the task at hand. There's not a right or wrong approach, there is only an inspired approach. If you want to get joy from your work, you need to bring joy to your work.

Successful enterprises do not shy away from people with stimulating thoughts that provoke emotions in others. Passion for what you do can lead to mastery. That's not to say that what you're currently doing is great and that with ten more years, you'll be a master. You could be screwing up royally, and no one is telling you. As a result, ten years from now you'll mistakenly think you're a master. Instead, you're likely to become obstinate, or worse obsolete. Don't fool yourself with complacency. You already know what you're good at and finding a place that promised to give you the ability to do that regularly is probably what drew you to your job in the first place. Maybe things have changed, and now there are new things you're expected to do that you're not very good at. Pay attention to your current state. Energy drains and energy uplifts are immediate clues to your level of satisfaction.

If bringing out your artist sounds like too much work for you; you're probably right. Take it easy and keep on slogging away at what you're doing. Count your blessings that you're still employed in this economy and that no one has noticed you yet. Save your money. Sock a lot away for your retirement because you're going to need it – probably sooner than you think.

On the other hand, if you're nodding your head in agreement because you're already doing something you love right now or this sounds remotely interesting to you because you remember how you once did, congratulations, you have many achievements ahead of you.

When you bring your artist to work, you challenge the current thinking. You don't go searching for problems, but you do offer solutions. Lots of them. Artists are creative. Creativity scares too many people. It needn't. Creativity is what moves people, institutions and nations forward. Forward movement is never a bad thing, though it's not always painless.

Our best thinking, innovation and ideas are in front of us, not behind us. Sure, we can refer to the past to act as prologue, but today we have additional knowledge and hindsight we didn't have yesterday. This is as true on the world stage as it is in your daily life. You have prior knowledge, you have opinions, and you know what works and what doesn't. You have intellectual curiosity. You like to tinker, question, invent and innovate. Bringing that to your work is bringing the artist to work. If you can't do that because your work environment won't allow it, challenge the work environment to change. If it can't, prepare to leave it for a better environment. It's okay; with it's ridged thinking that organization is not likely to last much longer anyway. Sooner or later you'll need something new.

Every inspirational guru since the dawn of man has said, "we are living in the best of times" and they've all been right. We keep getting better.

Yes, we have tremendous challenges. The world is the smallest it's ever been and it's causing people to become more factious than we've ever been. There are epic struggles between change and preservation. The extremes of both sides lack the imagination and tools to explore the possibilities of each. It's the artist who sees multiple perspectives and brings people together. Successful leaders know this. So if your working with widgets, or children, spreadsheets or coffee beans, miracle drugs or motor vehicles, now is not the time to do it the same way. How will you bring your artist to work?

Solve the Damn Problem

June 7, 2010

Being careful with your language can show sensitivity, compassion and at least some tolerance in an increasingly intolerant country. As a writer, words matter, that's why I believe we shouldn't sugarcoat what we face as a nation and as individuals. Let's not waste time calling things *formidable challenges* when they're *big problems*. America used to be able to solve big problems. As a nation, we routinely lived our values.

It's easy to be a bit romantic and forget about how horrible this nation used to be for women before suffrage or African Americans before civil rights, or homosexuals until very recently. How poorly we treated our elderly, the mentally ill, and non-land owners. History's canvas is sometimes painted with a lighter touch. Hangings were common in my beloved city of Boston, the carcasses of criminals left out to publicly rot. The Son's of Liberty tarred and feathered other human beings. A blind eye was cast in the slave trade.

We forget we were founded as a violent nation. We picked off British Regulars while hiding in the woods. At the time we were thought of as savages, a term still offensive to Native Americans, but we took pride in our actions as patriotic and character building. Yet, when used against us in quagmires like Iraq and Afghanistan we consider it barbaric.

The American spirit will always be divided between those who look at us being on the continent as a matter of 'Divine Providence' and those who consider the nation the melting pot and that our greatest strength is incorporating the best ideas from everyone.

Winston Churchill once said, "Americans will always do the right thing, after they have exhausted all the alternatives." It's in that vein of faith I remain hopeful for America, but today a large portion of our population is apathetic. They might be angry, but they're also lazy. Or they're active, but without a sense of purpose. I'm not so sure Americans are trying everything with the spirit we are expected to. It can be taxing, but civil debate and disagreement coupled with pragmatism and searching for common ground is what has served this nation well in the past. The problem today is, our tries seem to be halfhearted, or we save the passion for the detestability of our opponents; political or imagined.

We are not trying hard enough. We are thinking less, worrying more and outsourcing our leadership to other nations, or corporations. As individuals, we are all responsible for the eroding spirit and grit because we are complacently letting it happen. We celebrate the First Amendment by giving the microphones to crackpots then undermine the gesture by reporting the fear and hate they spout as fact rather than opinion. We are focused on symptoms and finding ways to coat, soothe, and relieve them rather than solving the problems that are making us ill. We moan and complain. We spend a lot of energy doing very little and here are some of our results so far:

- 30% of Americans are obese
- 1 Million American High School students drop out each year
- We carry a $16 Trillion Debt and growing
- We are #1 in Oil Consumption, #2 in Coal Consumption and #1 in Cocaine Consumption
- 2.3 Million of our citizens are incarcerated, giving us the largest prison population on the planet

We can do better. We must do better. We can begin by teaching our children and each other how to dream big, think profoundly, decide pragmatically and lead courageously.

There are no shortages of serious problems yearning to be solved. Pick one.

Below are steps to help you begin to solve the problems that are within your ability to solve. If it looks like too much work, have someone help you. Being defeated from within helps no one.

1. Write down the problem or challenge that you need to solve.

2. Describe the desired state that could exist without the problem.

3. Describe WHY that state is desired.

4. Create a specific and measurable goal to make your intention specific and real.

5. Set criteria on how to find solutions to the problem.

6. Generate a brainstorm list of alternative solutions.

7. Narrow the list and pick the "best few" options.

8. Assess each option's feasibility and potential risks versus gains.

9. Reach a tentative agreement with stakeholders of the problem.

10. Put some resources on a fall back plan.

11. Firm up the final decision and announce it to those affected.

12. Develop an action plan to go forward.

13. Implement the action plan with confidence, commitment and passion.

14. Review, assess and celebrate progress.

Problems are often very complex. Their solutions seldom have to be.

How Did You Get To Be So Awesome?

January 2010

Having a vision of success is only part of the equation of achievement; unfortunately, it's where too many people stop. They can see what they want so clearly that it hurts. Yearnings are fine as long as they move us forward. It's a different story if the vision we set for ourselves leads to feelings of regret or depression because we've not achieved them fast enough.

Some wonder what they're doing wrong, and why things never seem to work out for them. As a result, despondent people give up on their vision. What they should be doing is asking better questions. Keep your vision. I'd argue, the wilder the better.

If you created your own vision then you know deep down inside you're able to achieve it. Today, assume you already have. Now, figure out how you did it by asking, "**Forward Reflective Questions**" like, "Why am I so successful?" "How did I earn so much money?" Or "Where did I find this wonderful person?" As with your goal setting, be as specific as you can in your reflection.

Do you think if you ask questions like these, you're lying to yourself? You might not FEEL successful yet, so how could you ask such a question? It's easy. Because like Michelangelo's David, the person you want to be is already in there, you just need to get rid of the things that aren't serving you anymore. It's time to release the baggage that someone else unloaded on you and you've been carrying all these months or years.

Our mind is a powerful solution-seeking machine. It likes to find answers. Therefore, if you question why you're a failure, you'll get answers and you won't like them. It's better to question why you are a success in whatever you choose to pursue. The answers to those questions may also surprise you and they will unlock a way of thinking that will bring you closer to your vision with greater speed.

Angry People Are Boring

February 2010

There's anger in our nation and there's plenty to be angry about, however we should stop acting as though this is a new phenomena. As a nation, we were angry ten years ago and ten years before that. Take five random people and ask what they're angry about and at least four will tell you everything that's wrong with the world. Of those four, two will agree and two will think the other two are to blame. Be the fifth person. It's okay to get ticked off from time to time yet remain reasonable.

Have you spent time with angry people? They make a lot of noise, even when they pout and give the silent treatment you can hear the doors slamming and feet pounding and music blaring. They may incite some passive aggressive behaviors from you, like a meaningless post on Facebook. Eventually though, all angry people become boring and boring people ultimately are ignored.

Anger isn't bad. It's a clue that something is assaulting our core beliefs and values. If we don't respond to the feeling of anger, we run the risk of letting our beliefs and values atrophy. That's one of our nation's major threats.

When we're angry we make trigger reactions that are fueled by instinct. It's a quick gut check and a good survival mechanism. However, it's not meant to be our primary modus operandi.

At some point, if you want to affect change you need to shift from a reactive stance to a position of "respond-ability."

I'm sure you've witnessed two people quarreling. When we're not directly involved in the dispute it's often amusing to watch and listen to the irrational arguments and assertions each party makes and the huge leaps of logic they take. You can tell they're not hearing each other. They just want to be more right than their opponent.

Contrast that to an angry customer pitted against a well-trained customer service professional. The professional may mirror the irate customer but they also empathize. They're not using the primitive brain to react and counter react, they are responding by being thoughtful and creating a setting where cooler heads can arrive at a mutually satisfying solution.

Anger is fine, but at some point, you need to act responsible and lower your irrational, venomous rhetoric so you can get to work on fixing what's making you angry to begin with.

If you just stay mad, the adrenaline rush may be fun for you, but you quickly degenerate into a chronic whiner, and no one likes a whiner. **Whiners make crappy leaders**. That's the fundamental problem with the current political climate. We have a bunch of angry whiners who love to make a lot of noise and get attention because they equate that with leadership. It's not, it's gimmickry. People can't resist a freak show, they'll even spend money on it, but they quickly move on.

Leaders do things. Sometimes they make noise, sometimes they make mistakes; but they always **do** things. Are you part of the angry mass, upset about something within your control? Grab a mop and start cleaning up the mess instead of being angry about the size of the mop, or the floor, or the cleaning solution. Offer alternatives and lead people, or shut up and get over yourself, you're boring.

It's Obvious

Want to figure out what you're good at? Need to find a way to be useful to humanity? There's no shortage of books and programs to help you explore those questions. I'll save you a few hundred, maybe a few thousand dollars, and give you the answer. It's obvious.

Think for a moment about some of the best gifts you've received. They may have been meticulously wrapped and presented by someone who loved you. Maybe they wore a huge smile and brimmed over with confidence when they gave it to you because they knew they had found the perfect present for you and were excited to see you open it. It was probably something you hadn't asked for, hadn't even thought about. But they did. They thought about you and knew this was something you *had* to have. When you think back on it, they were right. It was perfect.

I remember one birthday my father gave me such a gift. I had been pinning for a VHS video camera for months and the box he handed me seemed to fit the dimensions, although heavier than I imagined. When I tore the wrapping open, I was crushed to see a silver Craftsman toolbox. I flipped the latch, hoping for some type of redemption, cassette tapes or batteries I could use. Inside were five or six individually wrapped smaller gifts; a hammer, screwdrivers and wrenches. That was over twenty years ago and I never got a VHS camera, but I still open that silver toolbox at least once a week to find some instrument to help rescue, fix or create something in my life. It and its contents, which have grown, have become one of my prized possessions.

We all start out with a special gift or two. I believe they were presented to us at birth from a higher power with that same enthusiasm and knowing smile, but maybe for you, it was someone else. As a blob of a kid, you didn't know what it was, but you gurgled and squealed, happy to receive it. The Universe didn't tell you how to use it, or even what it was. The wrapping was part of the gift. You had some time to guess what was inside by shaking it around a little and going through some trial and error to rule things out.

Some people unwrapped their present at a very young age, others waited until they were much older. After a lot of poking, prodding, staring and guessing, everyone eventually unwraps their gift, but not everyone knows what they've been given.

It's obvious.

Your gift is the thing you do well. It's your talent. The thing that comes so easy for you that you mistakenly assume everybody has it. They don't. Your gift is the thing that you do nearly effortlessly and without thought. It's frustratingly simple to uncover. You've probably been ignoring your gift because it has seemed too easy, not grand enough, or you haven't felt worthy because you've been tricked into thinking your gift needs to be complicated. Powerful gifts are not complicated. Your talent is easy to identify. Once you've identified your gift, don't be insulting. Use it. How you choose to use it is the present you pass along to others.

Autonomy, Responsibility, Scapegoating

People dislike the word accountable, probably because they associate it with blame. That shortsighted, glass half-empty perspective can hold you back. Autonomy, the freedom to make your own decisions, continues to rank among the top desires of people in their work life. Accountability is not, *Who's to blame?* it's *Who's responsible?* When you're responsible for something but decide not to act, that's called abdication, which is a fancy word for quitting. Autonomy without accountability is kind of silly.

I was once engaged to help on a project that had gone awry. I asked the team who was accountable for various assignments and told them it was their responsibility to find ways to fix the errors within their purview. I wasn't blaming them I was reiterating their duties. Senior management was skittish and said, "Don't you think you're being too rough? We're all in this together." That's great, but it was false. They permitted autonomy but not responsibility. Kind of silly, right?

On a separate occasion, the same organization had another undertaking that its leadership had abdicated. I didn't know any of the particulars when I was called in, other than their customer was ticked off. I took over the project and asked the role of each stakeholder. I told everyone I was the one ultimately responsible for the success or failure of the project, but they were responsible for their individual roles. Most people were relieved, because the target was off their back, and they had a new person to blame if things continued to go wrong. I held regular progress report meetings and when something stalled, the causal was evident to everyone.

During the first few meetings, the client was still angry, and they took it out on me. I didn't take it personally. Instead, I let them continue to vent their frustrations, which allowed me to learn their core concerns. I took their blame head on because I assumed accountability for the entire project. Some people called it falling on the sword. The status meeting communication was frequent and thorough, so everyone knew who or what truly hampered progress. As we worked closer with the client they began to share in some blame and by the end of the project, they were singing our praises. We moved from the cusp of being thrown out, to being named their provider of choice, because we chose accountability over scapegoating.

Being accountable isn't easy, which is why so many people shirk it. When you accept accountability it's empowering, and things do get easier. You have a choice. If things are not going well in your relationship or your finances, your current skill set, your health outlook or any other area of your life, are you going to use the government, the economy, the weather or your parents as a scapegoat for you? Blaming gets pretty boring. Taking responsibility, now **that's** exciting. You can actually do stuff.

Pick one or two things you've blamed on others and ask yourself, "For what part of this problem am I accountable?" Show some leadership. Accept responsibility and get to work on improving what's within your power to improve. You'll be pleasantly stunned by what you can accomplish.

Pelican Teamwork

My family and I visited Pier 39 in San Francisco. At my children's urging, we once again took a peak at the sea loins who have overtaken the docks and become an attraction all to themselves. We had visited them a few times over the course of the weekend and again, we joined the throngs of people cluttered at the edge of the pier. The seal lions, with their distinctive smell were in various stages of sleep and play, their guttural barks filling the early evening. Onlookers were thoroughly entertained by their antics. However, having seen them numerous times, my eyes drifted upward. I caught in the distance four birds circling closer and I soon realized they were pelicans. Although I have seen pelicans fly before, I marveled at how such an ungainly bird on the wharf can look so majestic in flight. It was about to get better.

I watched the unfolding vista in absolute awe as the summer sun was setting behind the Golden Gate Bridge and the hills of Sausalito. I noticed this initial set of four birds was suddenly joined by another group of seven. With each lap, the birds picked up another small flock overhead. Each group independently demonstrated perfect symmetry; wings in synchronicity the lead bird setting the pace, another one, just to the left and then the familiar "V" formation behind them. As each grouping of four or seven birds joined on, the larger flock seamlessly accepted them, forming a wider "V". Eventually there were twenty birds, their wings mimicking the waves beneath them.

They continued to circle overhead. Above the barking and noise of the jovial sea lions, these ungainly birds continued their work, undaunted and unnoticed by the scores of eyes, nearly all instead fixated on the blubbery show before them. The pelicans continued to circle quietly, their wings still in harmony and elegance. I noticed then as their "V" formation melded into a single row and they then began to dive toward the water's surface in a wave like manner, each scooping their bills one after the other. A precision fishing machine. Soon, twelve cormorants mirrored the technique.

The setting was breathtaking and reminded me of the Ken Blanchard phrase, "All of us are smarter than one of us." These pelicans, and the cormorants for that matter, illustrated the value of teamwork and an abundance mentality. Contrast the silent elegance, and precision integration soaring in the sky above to the barking, smelly seal lions that grunted and wheezed competitively for a space on a crowded dock that's not even theirs. Which team would you prefer to be on?

61 Positive Actions To Consider

You run around with one hundred things to do but feel like you don't get anywhere. Here are 61 positive actions that ought to move you in the right direction. That leaves you with 39 others to futz around with.

1. Write a note and mail it to someone. It's a nice thing to do and it forces you to think about someone else. You get to practice your penmanship and help support the post office by using a stamp. Everyone benefits from this small act.

2. Smile. Regardless of your current condition, there are a few things in life that still make you smile. Seek them out. Smile in the mirror. If nothing else, you'll experience the joy of being smiled at by someone attractive.

3. Laugh. Laughter helps you. It works muscles that are hard to reach any other way. It also shows you have a sense of humor. Find people or situations that give you such a belly laugh it hurts your sides. Bonus points if you pee a little.

4. Get in a good cry and get over it. Life is not always rosy and perfect. Even Martha Stewart spent time in jail. Bad things happen. Sometimes you hurt somebody and sometimes you're hurt. When everything feels out of your control, grab a pint of beer or ice cream and drown your sorrows. Stop trying to be so strong. Sometimes things suck. Cry until you're all out of tears and snot. Give yourself two hours, maybe a little more if you're particularly aggrieved. Then get over it. Brush yourself off and get back in the game.

5. Learn something. If you think you know everything, you're probably an idiot. In the grand scheme of things, even with the Internet, you don't know much. Develop your intellectual curiosity. It doesn't have to be stressfully ambitious. Maybe it's flipping a fried egg without breaking the yoke, or understanding someone else's point of view on some issue. It's good to stretch yourself too, so consider learning how to play a musical instrument, or speak Urdu. There's no shortage of things to learn.

6. Teach someone. Teaching helps you learn. It solidifies your thinking, and if you have a great student, challenges your thinking and makes you even better. To teach someone is one of the greatest gifts you can give to another human being.

7. Say thank you. Although it's egotistically healthy to expect things in life, it's polite to be appreciative when you get them. When you don't say thank you because you're too busy, too important or too careless, people think you're an ass -- and they're right.

8. Be okay being wrong. Some people relish being right. Full disclosure, one of my favorite sounds is when someone tells me, "You were right." It has a very appealing musical quality to me. I prefer being right, but I'm okay being wrong. Being fallible is a human condition. Being wrong, and smart enough to admit it, not only teaches you something, beside humility, it also endears you to others. It takes bigger guts to admit your mistakes than to blame others.

9. Hug. Don't be afraid of hugging. It's a beautiful demonstration of affection, respect, warmth, caring and understanding; things the world can continue to use more of. Increase your contribution.

10. Drink more water. It's good for you. It hydrates your brain, flushes toxins out of your system, and you're not getting enough. Flavor it if you must, but get eight ounces for every hour you're awake. Tomorrow you'll feel better than you do today.

11. Reassert your values. Look where you've spent your time and money over the last three months to learn what you currently value. Are you happy about that? If not, start acting in better alignment to the things you say you value.

12. Make a plan. At night, or in the morning, every day, once a week or once a month, plan what you're going to do. What do you want to have happen? What do you need to get done? Write it down and plan it out. A lousy plan surpasses no plan.

13. Do something off plan. Some people get a little too ridged with their planning and have no room left on their calendar. Be open to serendipity.

Have some flexibility to go off script from time to time. Have superior focus *and* peripheral vision.

14. Go out of your way to help someone. Everyone could use a little boost from time to time. Everyone faces a struggle, no matter where they fall on the socio-economic scale. You have time, treasure or talent that someone else could benefit from. Help other people when they need it, not when it's convenient for you.

15. Count your money. Always know how much you have. It's empowering. Sometimes it can be shocking, (positively or negatively), but it's always better to know, because the knowledge influences you to make better decisions.

16. Put 10% of your money aside. You're not saving enough. Yes, it's hard when times are tough and expense keep growing, but this habit helps you in the long run. Go extreme. Each night when you empty your pockets or set your wallet aside, count your money, put 10% in a jar or an envelope, and don't touch it. The first few times it will feel unnatural. Soon, it will be fun and you'll become as excited about saving money as you are about spending it.

17. Read something. If it's not a habit yet, make it one. Read every day. To get started, it doesn't matter what you read. Eventually, challenge yourself to read above your comfort zone, both in language and genre or perspective.

18. Learn a new word. An increase in vocabulary correlates to an increase in wealth. When you become aware of the meaning of words, you're more apt to use them correctly and judiciously. It improves your decision-making skills. When I was younger, my mother, sister and I randomly opened the dictionary, pointed to a word and used it for a week. I stupefied my third grade teacher when I told her I was shy in school, but loquacious at home.

19. Clean up your mess. Somewhere around you is a mess. Instead of complaining about it, clean it up. Loose papers, a sink full of dishes, scattered laundry. Stop staring at it and getting yourself all worked up. Clean it up and be done.

20. Donate some clothes. You have too many. Something is out of style, doesn't fit, or is ugly as sin. Give it away. Throw it in a bag and sneak off to one of those donation boxes or regift it to an appreciative friend or family member with great fanfare. It doesn't matter how you do it, just get rid of it.

21. Trade habits. Save your time trying to break a bad habit. Instead, decide on something good you want to do, (pick any number on this list) or choose a "less-bad" habit to replace it with.

22. Break a sweat. Some hate to sweat and some love it. Do something that creates enough exertion to make you sweat. Don't endanger your health, but move faster than you do now.

23. Save your will power for later. Studies suggest we each have a limited reserve of will power; some have more, some less. It's used during the day and replenished with sleep. If you exhaust your will power during the day, you'll be less likely to call upon it in the evening when you may wish you had better judgment. Two options; give in to your morning weakness so you don't succumb to evening temptation, or plan your day ahead of time and determine where you will say yes and no, and stick to it.

24. Decide how much, and by when, for three important things. When you know how much, you've set a metric or success measure. When you know by when, you've set a deadline. Now you have three goals, instead of three wishes.

25. Marvel at something bigger than yourself. Justifiable arrogance or cockiness doesn't bother me too much, but egomaniacal behavior is abhorrent. To guard against this, visit nature or contemplate something bigger than yourself. When I lived in Boston, I liked to walk by the John Hancock building and look at my reflection in the glass. In one pane I felt sure of myself, but when I let my eyes gaze upward 60 stories, I couldn't help but feel insignificant. I feel the same when I glance at the moon. For thousands of years humans have looked up at it in wonder. In my lifetime, people have been there and back. You've got to know where you fit, and then explore the boundaries.

26. Complete something. Find something incomplete and finish it. There's a project you started, months, maybe years ago, still sitting there waiting for you. It could be a book you began writing, an engine you're rebuilding in the garage, an afghan you're crocheting, a piece of IKEA furniture you gave up on. Roll up your sleeves and get it done. Finish something and celebrate your success.

27. Walk. You're not doing enough of this. Park farther away, take more stairs, walk around the block, or beach, or park. Move your body.

28. Oppose something. There is something you are vehemently against, but you've been politely silent. It's an opinion someone has been spouting off, or an important issue that's not going the direction you want it to. Speak up, act and oppose it. Rock the boat if you have to. You have the right to be heard. Speak with your voice, your pen, or your feet.

29. Be for something. Being for something doesn't always illicit the passion as being against something does, but it has the advantage of being action in the affirmative.

30. Fix something. A flickering light, a dripping faucet, a relationship with a loved one. Something in your surroundings is currently broken. Fix it, on your own or with the help of others. Now.

31. Create something. Make something you can point to and say, "I did that." Decorate a room, make a killer presentation, write a poem, build a house. You decide the scope and scale, but get started and then complete it (see #26).

32. Hold someone's hand. Two hands together feels powerful. It creates a connection and solidifies a bond. Be it intimate or casual, lifesaving or comforting, holding hands puts you in touch with humanity.

33. Prepare. Life happens. Are you ready for it? An opportunity, disasters, events on the calendar, and the unforeseeable alike, something is constantly happening. The better prepared you are to meet it head on; the more likely you'll handle it successfully.

34. Ask. People enjoy being asked. They won't always give you the answer you want, but asking at least gives them the option. Asking trumps telling in creating respect. Asking also greatly enhances your chances of getting what you want.

35. Organize. Something in your life is in disarray. It might be as simple as your sock drawer, or where you keep your bills. Maybe, your thinking is cluttered. Make the time to get things in order. You will feel better and productive.

36. Act on purpose. Do you know what you're doing and why? Most people don't bother to ask simple questions of themselves. You ought to, multiple times a day. Is what you're doing moving you in the direction of your dreams or is it deferring them? Adjust your course.

37. Show gratitude. People sometimes think they are owed something. Typically, the less grateful believe they are owed the most. Abandon the self-righteous attitude you sometimes carry with you. Shut up for a few minutes and be appreciative of all you have and all you have learned.

38. Treat yourself. There's no need to go hog wild. You don't need to throw a parade for tying your shoes, but reward yourself for accomplishing something of significance instead of shrugging it off as no biggie.

39. Treat someone else. When you notice other people and the good they are doing, it's natural, and smart to show your appreciation. Find people doing good things and treat them with something they would like.

40. Put off procrastination. Procrastination is perhaps your biggest enemy, stop giving it so much of your time. It keeps you away from accomplishment.

41. Know the difference between dichotomy and hypocrisy. Dichotomy is acknowledging some complex systems require two opposing forces to work properly, (you breathe in and out). Hypocrisy is claiming one thing but acting in opposition.

42. Watch School House Rocks. Please, get a basic understanding of the founding of the

United States and how the government works. (as well as math and grammar). I'm personally tired of bloviating elected representatives who don't know the basics. It's not entirely their fault. We the people, put them there, probably because we were ignorant or fell prey to their tortured logic. Get a minimal primer and smarten up. This stuff's important.

43. Know your preferences. Stop living with your default settings. Advocate for what you want. You won't always get it, but at least try.

44. Vote. Every time there is an opportunity to voice your opinion and preferences, do it. It's an incredible empowering feeling. If you have doubts as to how vital and important it is, look at how hard people work to get your vote, or try to subvert it. Trying to dissuade another from voting is a despicable and reprehensible act. Elections have consequences. Take your responsibility seriously. Learn what you must to make an informed decision, then make it, and then make sure your vote is counted.

45. Apologize properly. We've all heard crappy apologies. They included the words "if" and "but". Those aren't apologies; they are noisy and useless public relations exercises. A proper and sincere apology meaningfully fills in the blanks. "I'm sorry. I feel _____. I _____, and take responsibility for the harm that's caused. I acted in a way that's not consistent with who I want to be. I'm going to make amends for the damage I've done by _____."

46. Slow down and think. We are being inundated with information from a variety of sources. With all the outside stimuli, we tend to react to uncertainty by hunkering down with what we think we already know instead of thoughtfully pursuing a rational alternative to the circumstances in front of us. Gather a variety of information from different sources. Look at things from a historical, political, social, economic and humanistic perspective rather than regurgitating someone else's opinion.

47. Speed up and act. Colin Powell has said, once the probability of success of a decision is between 40% and 70%, make the decision. Acting with less than 40% is careless and if you wait until it's greater than 70%, the opportunity will have probably already passed.

48. Know geography. Know where in the world you are. Know who's around you. Know what the other side of the world looks like. Geography has a great influence and it matters. If you struggle to find where you are on a map, why would you expect people to want to follow you to where you say you want to go?

49. Be Awesome. You can change how you feel anytime you want. Choose to be awesome.

50. Get Inspired. Listen to upbeat music, inspirational speeches, sermons, podcasts or books.

51. Get Happy. First, pay attention to what you regularly complain about, then shut up and fix it or just shut up. Your complaining is annoying. Next, identify five positive people and spend more time with each of them. Hanging out with happy people, helps make you happy. Still struggling? Write down the things that make you happy and then figure out how to spend more time with the things and people that lift your spirits.

52. Help Someone On Their Terms. Ask someone, "What one thing can I do for you that will most help you make a positive difference?" and then help them.

53. Figure out why you're still here. Ask yourself, "Why am I still working here?" Is it for personal development, because of enriching experiences with others or to work on leaving a legacy? If it's not clear, go someplace where it is.

54. Draw a picture of success. You don't have to pull out the crayons, you can write it down if you prefer. Create a repeatable compelling vision and sense of purpose and then, ask for help. You'll probably need a hand, and people like being asked.

55. Find the upside to your biggest challenge. Do that, and you've nearly conquered the thing because your fear will turn to purpose.

56. Be a child. Can you remember what you always want to be when you grew up? Why? What about now? List your ten best excuses for not pursuing your dreams. Let them stare back at you and mock you. Then turn them into an action plan and cross them off as you work to eliminate your barriers.

57. List your top three accomplishments. You've done some good things. Remind yourself of them.

58. Have a sense of overwhelming optimism. You can still be a realist. An optimistic realist is more fun to be around than a pessimistic realist.

59. Ignore or crush any apathy or negativism you encounter. They're out there, you can't avoid them, but just like pests, you can minimize your exposure. Keep a lid on the things they feed off so they don't return.

60. Recognize people for the good things they do. Don't stop at just thinking about it, actually thank people. Praise progress, even it it's approximately right. They don't hear it enough.

61. Believe in yourself and get to work. Justified confidence is great. Even unjustified confidence gives your spirits a boost. Sitting back in the glow of greatness is arrogant and will dim fast. Use your confidence, real or imagined, to work on the things that are important to you.

Nobody Wants to Wait 10 Years for Your Story

Everyone has projects they would like to get to, but life seems to get in the way. Most often, that takes the form of procrastination. Sometimes, it's because you truly have been too busy, but if you're going to be honest with yourself, too busy is code for, poor time management, or prioritization based on the needs of other people.

A project typically lays dormant because of fear, uncertainty or doubt. *Can it be finished? What will it look like? Will I/you/they like it enough? What if no one else likes it?* These are all reasonable fears, but they hold you hostage, and *that* is unreasonable. If you're going to feel those emotions anyway, doesn't it make sense to get them over with?

I know, sometimes it takes time to erect a statue or build a new park. Some things can't be rushed. Ideas need to ferment, the Muses need to sing in perfect harmony and the planets need to align, but for how long ... really?

I'm not exempt. I have no shortage of half-baked prose sucking up disk space and file cabinets, but I'm talking about the projects you're 'actively' working on, or telling people you are. There are countless tales about authors who have slaved over their novel for years. Sometimes they finish it on their deathbed and sometimes death beats them to their final period.

When I hear those stories I often wonder, *what the hell took them so long*? What got in the way? Sometimes a war, sometime booze, often depression. Believe me, I get it. Debilitating things in life can keep you from working on what you tell everyone you want to be working on, but let's be brutally honest, nobody wants to wait ten years for your book. You're supposed be a storyteller, not a tease.

If you're a writer, write the damn thing. If you're an artist, paint the damn thing. If you've got a passion project, finish it. Otherwise, what good is it to the rest of the world? You undoubtedly had plans for it to begin with, what happened?

It's now generally accepted that productivity helps to create happiness. So, it stands to reason that those who wallow over the lack of progress in their project, primarily due to their unproductive behavior, won't be particularly happy. To me, this is one of life's tragedies. You've got enough of a gift, the skill, the passion, heck, maybe all three, to have gotten something started. Now finish it. Stop with your excuses. Keep your commitments to yourself and move on.

Wisdom from the Father and Son

October 2005

I attended a seminar where the reflective question was posed, "How do you remind yourself that God is present in your workplace and how does that awareness change the way you work?"

It was an interesting question and I must admit I wasn't particularly happy with the answer I came up with. I didn't think I reminded myself very often if at all, and that seemed like something I should rectify, but I wasn't sure how. When I returned to my office I scoured my desktop for some icon that could act as an unobtrusive spiritual symbol. My laptop, docking station and monitor took a vast amount or real estate. Stacks of papers to file, act on or route robbed even more. What little shelf space I had was committed to books and business tchochkies. Before long, pressing matters tore me away from my search.

While at home my young son, to his great amusement, continued to pick up and throw rubber balls at me. This was a fun game we had been playing for several days but in a flash it became much more significant. As he ran after me, arm cocked and ready to catapult another ball toward me, he gleefully said, "Here Daddy, here." At that moment I interpreted what he was saying as, "*Hear* Daddy, *hear*."

Instantly I recalled back a few years to a joyful family reunion. The occasion was my father's birthday, (for that matter, my daughter's too.) He rose to give a little speech, a recollection of what someone had shared with him as a younger man. He said words to the effect,

"In life we find ourselves juggling any number of balls in different sizes. There is career, finances, health, perhaps new business ventures, schooling or needless worrying. All of these things are made of rubber. If one drops because of neglect or a miscalculation, it can bounce back. However, there is one ball that represents family and it is made of crystal. This ball requires the most vigilant attention, because if it should fall due to neglect or miscalculation it will shatter and can not be replaced."

With moistness in my eyes, I gave my surprised son a big hug before he could pelt me with another ball.

On my desk sits a picture of my family in a crystal frame. Alongside of it I have placed a rubber ball I tend to throw or squeeze when the day turns tense. The two items work in concert to remind me that God is indeed present and he came to me through my father and my son.

Who Do You Wish More People Could Meet?

Was there ever a person in your life who you wanted to introduce to other people, but now it's too late? For me it was my grandfather. He was of another era. To hear his voice, cadence and dialect you'd think you were like watching an old Frank Capra or George Cukor movie from the 1940's. He was always ready with amusing stories, riddles or a practical joke.

Growing up we would visit nearly every Sunday and spend a few hours with him and my grandmother. One of my favorite memories of him, and I learned one of his favorite of me too, was the day he was pitching tennis balls to my wiffle ball bat in the back yard. I was fairly young, I was dismal, and I was getting frustrated with myself. Embarrassed, I collected several of the missed balls that were scattered by my feet and tossed them back to him so we could try again. A few rolled behind him and into the bushes forcing him to crawl in to retrieve them. My frustration grew; I couldn't even toss a ball right. I was determined to hit the next pitch with all my might.

He brushed himself off, paused for a moment, asked if I was ready and then hurled the brightly colored ball at me. I concentrated and hit it perfectly on the fat part of the bat with an exploding crack. Literally, the 'ball' exploded into hundreds of little pieces! At first, I was scared, what had I done now? Then I was bewildered as my grandfather began laughing heartily, like a mischievous Santa Claus. As we walked toward each other he held out his hand and revealed three large unripe crabapples, the same coloring as the balls he had been pitching me. He had switched them when he was in the bushes. He was just as amused with himself, as he was proud of me for finally getting a hit, squarely and forcefully, with a smaller object to boot. My expression seared itself on his memory. From that point on he would periodically begin laughing spontaneously during our visits and retell the story for the next twenty or so years.

    I loved when he told stories. They could be from his childhood or from a recent visit to the doctor, he always had an anecdote or quip. During our visits, he would hold court from his leather chair in the corner of the living room, or in the dining room sitting in the only armed chair. In the den he would faithfully watch the Red Sox or Patriots during the era when they were contenders but not yet regular champions.

    One of the saddest days of my life was helping him into the car at the funeral of my aunt, his youngest daughter. His sudden sobs were unexpected, heartbreaking and profound. In time, the stories, riddles and jokes returned even as his health began to decline. We were fortunate to have him grace this earth for nearly a century. Although he has been gone for several years now, whenever I hear a story or riddle well told, or witness a prank well played, I think of him and smile. Lately, I find myself remembering him and wishing more people could have met him and benefitted from his humor and class.

Who do you know that you wish more people could meet? How many people are being introduced to you? Share your gifts freely; the world will be better for it.

It's Your Fault. There, I Feel Better.

It's easy to lay blame when things don't go right. People blame the weather for how they're feeling. They blame the economy for their own financial situation. Schoolyards, boardrooms and the halls of Washington reverberate with outrage as people try to assign blame to someone else. It's easier. It's easier to dispense blame than to accept accountability. Some people in the world have two viewpoints, yours and mine. When things go wrong, the fault is yours. When things go right, the credit is mine. Blame helps aid this belief. When I blame, I am able to shift accountability and shirk responsibility. Whew, what a relief. Unfortunately, I also give up power and leadership credibility. If I exert any effort to blame someone other than myself for some event, I empower him or her and weaken me.

When we blame someone, we are declaring that the responsibility was his or hers and it was misused. To be clear, there are times in our lives when this is empirically true. We see people squirm and contort all sorts of stories to shed the skin of responsibility they're supposed to wear. And more often than not, how do they respond? By blaming others. Watch any Sunday morning news program for ample examples.

Why are we, the most freedom loving people, so regularly ready to give up our power? It's because responsibility scares most of us. What if we screw up? People might blame us.

There are two ways to interrupt this vicious cycle. One is to accept blame that is rightfully yours. You can probably share it with someone else, for few are blameless, but it's better to take it alone. Accepting responsibility knocks the breath out of blame. Accept it; fix what you can and move on. If you dwell on it, you are just perpetuating the blame on yourself. What a waste.

The second way to begin eliminating the destructive power of blame is to overcompensate with its opposite, praise. Do you feel you are getting too much praise in your life? Do you get too much recognition for all the good things you do everyday? Some may say they don't need praise. I say, they just don't *realize* they need it. Do you feel like you are receiving more blame than praise? What are you finding more, fault or admiration with others? Even if you are not speaking the words, your mind is either assigning blame or praise, while you wait in line, read an article, watch the news, listen to the radio, attend a lecture or rally, or sip a drink at a bar. You can't turn off these thoughts but you can ensure your focus is more on praise and what's going right with your world and less on blame and what's going wrong.

Write Anyway

There is a growing contingent of people who believe writer's block is the writer's fancy way of making laziness or procrastination sound more "arty" and even admirable. It's a kind of creative martyrdom.

"I want to write...I need to write...I just can't do it right now. The muse's are being too cruel."

Sounds good. But it makes me yawn.

Yes, the blank page, or even the next paragraph has from time to time vexed anyone who has had the urge to write. Sometimes it feels like you've run out of things to say. You're washed over by a wave of anxiety that maybe you're done, there's nothing left in you. Perhaps you feel anger. A wall has been erected separating you from your creative genius, denying you the wit and spellbinding prose you had imagined. I suppose you could call THAT writer's block. The thing is, it takes more than that to stop a writer. A writer writes anyway. It might be crap or it might be lofty. It doesn't matter, because it's written. That's better progress than all the bemoaning coming from those who haven't spilled any ink.

A writer writes.

That's not to say things don't keep writers from writing, but that's always the writer's choice An argument with a loved one can ruin your day, or it can inspire a character's rage. Feeling sullen or ill can keep you from the keyboard, or that keyboard may be your therapy.

I'm not interested in the plight of those who say they write, but don't. To me the one who struggles over which words to cut or add, or feels pain over tone or tempo is far more engaging than one who laments that the writing gods aren't favoring them today.

Give me a break.
A writer writes.
I've fallen down on my latest novel. I've not picked it up to edit it since that dreadful chapter twelve got under my skin. I'm not blocked. I'm chicken shit. I'm a damn good writer, usually, and could fix it in thirty minutes, if I sat down and faced it. Instead, I've written other things. Poems, business articles, newsletters. I've not stopped writing. I've stopped working on that project, and it's pissing me off. That's my responsibility. Not the kids who want to play, not the loved one who provoked a draining argument, not the economy that fills me with financial tension. No, righties, it's not even Obama's fault. It's mine.

A writer writes, that's the thing that makes a writer different from everyone else. Don't be a hack, but the next time you bleat about not writing, at least put it in an email and send it to yourself so you will have written *something*.

My Leadership Point of View

By sharing my leadership point of view, you'll have a better understanding of who I am as a leader and artist and what I stand for. You'll get insight on where I'm coming from and how I think.

There are four philosophies you should know about me right up front.

- I love the study of leadership.

- I have high expectations and high hopes for people.

- I'm more interested in strengths than I am in weaknesses.

- Poor leadership decisions don't just tick me off; they motivate me to find better ones and to foster the leader within others.

Background

When I was a child I was ambidextrous. Because I had equal comfort I often switched between my left and right hands mid-sentence or in the middle of drawing a circle. This befuddled my teachers so they told me I had to choose a hand because they felt it was interfering with my school work. I picked my left and that seems congruent with my lifelong habit of choosing the more difficult path.

A few years later my parents got a divorce, although I don't think it had anything to do with my hand choice. My school work suffered anyway and my teachers felt it better for me to be placed in a "slower" class. I don't know if you remember those Resource Centers, beautifully named but socially ostracized places. I was put in a room with other "slow" kids. When we were released to join the rest of the students in easier subjects like art and gym you couldn't help but feel like a second class citizen. That went on for about six years and my mild dyslexia didn't help me to feel any better about myself.

I wanted to enter high school without the "help" of the resource center. I recall the first grade I received. It was for social studies and I got a "C" on my assignment. The teacher asked to meet with me after class and he explained that he graded me a "C" originally but later received a note from the Resource Center people; I guess I was on some sort of watch list. He said he could up it to a "B" based on their scale if I wanted him to. I didn't give it a second of thought before I told him I'd take the "C" because how else was I going to improve if I wasn't held to the same standard as everyone else? He seemed impressed with that and I was never bothered from the Resource Center people again.

Since then I've be attracted to the leaders and artists who focus on people's strengths. I learned to intertwine the values of strength and creativity from my parents. I don't dwell on life's hurdles. Instead, I focus on the talents and gifts we have to clear those hurdles.

I have a thirst for making a difference. Using insightfulness and creativity, I'm happiest when I can lead and inspire others to maximize their strengths and continuously improve themselves, their organization or our society, by bringing the powers of vision, passion and action. I believe this helps positively energize our nation and contributes to greater peace, prosperity, fun, understanding, responsibility and liberty in the world. I do this by regularly focusing on the **four pillars of my mission**.

1. Make a Positive Difference in the lives of others.
2. Strive to Lead and Inspire through my words and deeds.
3. Maximize the Strengths of others by using my own.
4. Continually Improve and Contribute to a "more perfect union".

I enjoy being an inspiration to people who in turn inspire themselves. I like to help others find their strengths and see what they have to offer our joint endeavor.

I want to help you find your vision or purpose. If you've already found it, that's great. I want to help you clear the obstacles off your path so you can reach your goals.

I do this partly for selfish reasons. I like how it infuses me with energy. It forces me to take my focus off myself, and put it on others, the way a servant leader should. It also gives me the opportunity to combat the damaging effects of poor leaders, influencers, and others who abuse their enormous power either through intent or ignorance.

What does helping bring out the best in people and having a clear goal look like? Think of President John Kennedy and his crazy idea of landing on the moon. He said;

"We choose to go to the moon in this decade and do the other things, not because they are easy, but because they are hard; Because that goal will serve to organize and measure the best of our energies and skills; Because that challenge is one that we're willing to accept, one we are unwilling to postpone and one we intend to win."

Humankind had been staring up toward the sky for thousands of years wondering about the moon. One day not that long ago, one of us said, let's do it, let's go there within ten years — and we did it! A fascinating feat that illustrates that **just about anything is possible with vision, passion, action and a deadline.**

I like to measure things, less to see shortfalls but instead to see what we're capable of doing and to build our credibility. I love to see the charts and graphs of goals and measurements of success; to see the results of common things in uncommon ways. I'm an observer, deliberative and analytical. I used to read American Demographics magazine for pleasure, so that should gives you some clues.

I am in a constant state of learning and application when it comes to leadership. Sometimes this can come across as tinkering, although I prefer the word refinement. Either way, it's with the best of intentions. I focus on strengths instead of weaknesses. Yes, sometimes weaknesses need to be addressed, but to overcome them I discover what can be done, versus what can't. I lead toward the future not from the past. I measure and monitor with success metrics; managing by fact, not by whimsy.

Here are a few things you can expect from me in our interactions:

- Two questions asked equally often, "Why?" and "Why not?"
- A quest for continuous improvement, to make good things great things.
- Measures for success, setting you up to win.
- The testing of assumptions, tasks, and decisions against the Vision or Objective.
- A greater interest in strengths, not irrelevant weaknesses.
- An abundance mentality that will push you to explore possibilities.
- An irritation with poor leadership decisions, be they my own or others.

And here's what I expect from you if you want to build a beneficial relationship:
- Be open to new or alternative approaches.
- Ask me, "So what?" or "Who cares?" to keep me focused.

- Give seemingly "crazy ideas" a chance to breathe.
- Support vetted processes that we prove work.
- Give and receive education easily.
- Call BS, BS.
- Have a sense of humor about yourself, the world and me.

I believe everyone has the capacity to become a leader, and it's the responsibility of each of us to identify that special talent we possess and to pursue it relentlessly.

While you make your mark and decide what you want to be positively remembered for during your time here, know, feel and act like you make a difference, because you do. That's why I'm committed to helping talented leaders and artists find the a-ha within. So, how can I help you today?

Stop Wasting Your Talent

The average person spends more time and money on activities that contribute to their personal detriment than to their personal development. Luckily, you're not average.

Leaders, artists and entrepreneurs surround themselves with positive people who uplift them and challenge them to even greater levels of accomplishment. They never ask, "When is it enough, when can I finish?" because they know it is as much about the journey as it is about the destination. They are devoted to learning and looking at the world differently in order to achieve their goals and aspirations.

You know this to be true, but maybe you have an uncertainty over your vision. Perhaps you've been feeling frustrated, overwhelmed and discouraged while trying to complete someone else's goals instead of your own and your dreams keep getting deferred. It's not their fault, it's yours. They're your dreams, goals, and aspirations. You created them. You own them. They're your responsibility. What's holding you back?

Imagine it's six months from today. What you would feel like if you have achieved great strides in your goals? What has to have happened for you to feel happy with your progress, personally and professionally?

People say they don't have enough time or money to achieve their goals. It's that kind of thinking that continues to keep them from their dreams.

Some people sabotage themselves. They do all the "right" things and then panic. What if they succeed? What would happen next? It freaks them out, so instead of one or two more steps toward greatness, they settle for mediocrity.

Maybe your life is working out fine. Maybe your relationships are strong, your career is on the right track and you know how to celebrate life's achievements.

Or ... you could be searching for something more.

If you're struggling to find, set or get your great goals it's probably in part, because you're not holding yourself accountable for the little steps you need to do to achieve big results. Start doing that, or find someone who can help you.

How I Became a Recovering Quitter

I'm a recovering quitter. Several years ago, I felt trapped in my management job, but I needed to support my family. I called it burnout, but then realized it was wrong to blame my attitude on burnout when I was acting like an arsonist. I had to learn how to stay when what I really wanted to do was quit.

I knew that to change my attitude, I had to change my mind. I started looking for the positive lesson within every aspect of my job that I had viewed negatively, and decided to see each situation as a challenge to be solved instead of a problem. I asked myself, "What do I really want?" The answer didn't come right away because I was so entrenched in all of the things I didn't want.

Then I asked myself, "Why are you still here?"

When people want to quit, they quit. I realized there must be some reason people stay on a job when they aren't engaged—some benefit—or they would be gone. I found three reasons:
  1. To work on personal development
  2. To enrich others
  3. To focus on something bigger than yourself

I realized that as a manager, I had the potential ability to play a role in other people's lives and it was my own choice whether that experience would be positive or negative. That appealed to me.

Once I was reenergized and reengaged with my coworkers, I found myself better able as a leader to help those who I could see were mentally quitting by asking them these questions:

1. What's going right?
2. What do you really want?
3. What's keeping you here?
4. What will you do in the meantime?

Since people don't stay in the same position—or even industry—for their whole career, if you as a leader can help them get to the next place faster, you will both be more engaged and more productive.

Be A Leader Even When You Don't Feel Like It

There are plenty of un-leaderlike moments I could pick from, but there's one, as I think about it, which has haunted me for quite some time—so I offer my leadership "confessional" to you today.

Several years ago, I worked for a corporation that really valued continuous learning improvement and development for all its employees. I definitely benefited from it and it was terrific. But it was time to move on—it was my last week and I had a short-timer's attitude. One of my colleague's direct reports came to me, because her boss wasn't available, and asked me for some help with a scheduling conflict. It seems he had signed up for class work that interfered with his work schedule. The coursework didn't really have much to do with the job she was doing or with the immediate goals she had shared, so it frustrated me—plus, as I mentioned, I had short-timer's disease. That's really no excuse, but it's the one I used. Ultimately, I said to the employee, "No one told you to sign up for this class," which was a horrible response from me, a manager and a leader, to someone who had come looking for help.

It haunted me for some time. I tried to solve it but it was a little too soon and had cut a little too close to the bone for her.

I think the lesson in this is that when you are a leader, you need to act like a leader—because people are watching you, whether they are your direct reports or not. Leadership is about leading, even when it's not convenient or on your timetable, or even when it's about problems that you really don't have any desire to solve. If you are a leader, and people are looking at you and coming to you as a leader, you should be acting as a leader.

How to Keep Yourself From Burning Out

I once worked with an organization where people started vanishing. Now, some of that was due to their own accord—they moved on to bigger and better things. The vast majority, however, were being laid off, one at a time, so it was kind of a drip, drip, drip.

At a time like this, you don't really realize that work starts piling up for those who remain. During that time you kind of get a sense of "survivor's guilt" – wow, all those people aren't here anymore, they're out of a job, they're not in the same environment . You feel bad and guilty that you're still employed—until you start feeling kind of stressed and burned out because of all the extra work that you're doing. Then, those nice feelings turn into a sort of resentment, and a sense that the lucky ones got out and I'm stuck doing all this work.

That may be true. There's a lot of additional work to do. But I challenge you to take a contrarian point of view that I painfully had to get through to get to this place. It's about attitude. The sense of blaming things on burnout when you're the arsonist and you're doing it to yourself is just not appropriate. It's like writers who complain about writer's block—one of the best ways to solve that is to write. I think you need to adjust your attitude.

There are a few tactics I have come across, or warning signs. One is to beware of the three donkey day. Over the course of your day, if you come across three separate people who are being particularly nasty to you and you don't like their attitude—if there are three, it's probably time for you to do a little self reflection— because it's probably you who is being the donkey. Step back and take a look.

The second thing to remember, somewhat related, is that attitudes are contagious and you want to make sure you're catching the right one. It's very tempting to feed into negative things that are going on around you, but avoid that. Find people who are positive, who are finding the good things. Sometimes it might involve being outside of work to do that—that's okay. Just find that great attitude. Think about three to five people you might want to start hanging around with more often.

The third thing is what I call the power question—asking a coworker, "What's the one thing I can do for you that will most help make a positive difference?" You might be thinking, What? I have to take on another thing? I can't do that. The difference here is that it's something that will make a difference to them. And by reaching out and helping, you're going to feel better. You're actually working on something worthwhile and not trivial, and not complaining about things.

The thing is, we are capable, as human beings, of handling an awful lot of true hardship. Our minds are built around problem solving and not whining. So if we keep that perspective, we are able to get through these rough periods of doing more with less.

Let's Eradicate Despondency

When I was in college, I returned home one Friday for a long weekend. I met my mom in the afternoon, and she told me about a troubling sight she had seen earlier in the day. A school bus had stopped beside her, and the faces of sullen and despondent teenagers filled every visible window.

"They're kids," she said. *"On a Friday afternoon. Going home for a long weekend."* Her voice was soaked in sadness. *"This is supposed to be an exciting and optimistic time in their lives. They shouldn't look like they have the weight of the world on their shoulders."*

We lived in an affluent town, and although teen angst can run deep and shouldn't be trivialized, I doubt few on that bus had any want unmet.

My mom reminisced over the joy she had felt as a young woman, enthusiastic over what each tomorrow held in store for her. She wistfully hinted that bringing a surplus of unbridled exuberance into adulthood helps because it takes an increasing amount of effort to retain or recapture it after sustaining the random blows life inevitably throws your way.

A quarter of a century has passed since then, and the mournful expression on my mom's face remains seared in my memory. I couldn't articulate it at the time, but on that day a seed was planted that took root and intertwined with my mission to create a movement of leaders, artists and entrepreneurs committed to eradicating despondency from the faces and hearts of the disillusioned.

When you see the sad, slack, bovine expressions of listless figures through a window, or in your bathroom mirror, you're not looking at purposeful people motivated by an exciting and worthwhile goal. You're seeing disillusionment, worry and fear. These are horrible expressions to have painted across anyone's face, let alone the young. Discouragement and demoralization do not suddenly appear. They are signs of erosion, put there by constant exposure to negative elements which not only rob people of their faith and ingenuity, but also insidiously subvert fledging talents with ridicule, disdain, or worse, indifference.

Consider now, the teens who carried those gloomy expressions my mom saw, are today in their early 40s. Some may have recaptured the joy and enthusiasm my mother spoke of, but many, dare I guess most, have not. Today they are your doctors, bankers, teachers and professors perhaps educating you or your children, police officers and city planners, elected officials, and cubicle dwellers who wait in long lines for their first cup of coffee in the morning and lean on the car horn and swear at no one in particular in the early evening.

I have always hated poor leadership, and I'm sure you'd agree, people who are disillusioned, discouraged and chronically disappointed with where they are in life make poor leaders. They can systematically erode the optimistic possibilities held by others. And if they are in a position of influence, they are, through ignorance more than intent, creating a new generation of poor leaders. That cycle must stop.

I believe happiness and purposefulness come about by the active pursuit of a worthy goal, therefore if you want to be happy you should never be without a great goal.

I believe most people know what they want to contribute to society, but lack the confidence to pursue their dreams.

I believe great listeners create great leaders, artists, and entrepreneurs and when you learn to listen, particularly to yourself, epiphanies become common, and it's as easy to find the aha within as it is to find a blade of grass. You simply need to know where to look.

I believe accountability raises both your game and your aim. You achieve more when you're held accountable for your decisions and your actions.

I believe, with your help, we can eradicate despondency from the faces and hearts of the disillusioned and dissipate its corrosive effect on the world at large.

Imagine if every woman, every man, and every child you know had at least one great goal that they were actively working toward every day? The buzz of energy produced from such productivity, collaboration and purposefulness would do more than illuminate cities it would illuminate minds long shrouded under a fog of doubt. It would raise hope, lift spirits, and propel those with a success mindset ever forward. To solve what others thought unsolvable. To achieve what all but a few thought unattainable. To refuse the deferment of dreams long-held, or thoughts long held silent. To try, to fail, to try again, without stigma or scorn.

I believe such a place and time are possible. We won't ever live in a world without conflict, but we can't call it living if it's in a world without goals. The best we could do then is exist, and merely existing is not good enough for me, and I doubt it is for you.

If you have a great goal, I would love to know what it is.

If you're working on a great goal, I'd love to know how it's going.

And if you need help finding or working on a great goal for yourself or your organization I'd love to talk with you.

If you can only take baby steps toward the direction I'm headed, do so by sharing this message with every woman, every man, and every child you know who needs to find one great goal. Tell them it's possible.

Thank you and may you continue to advance confidently in the direction of your dreams, live the life you've imagined for yourself and help others along the way.

Where are the Poets?

Where are the poets, the dancers
the dreamers who make things come true?
Where are the leaders, and believers
and the folks who know what to do?

Why are there quarrels
and debate
over things of nonsense
rooted in nothing but hate?

Why are there cracks in solemn foundations,
born forth from greed?
They sprout and spread persistently
like rats, or lice or weeds.

What are the lyrics
that makes a nation pause?
What notes must be strung together
for each of us to admit our flaws?

Where are the engineers, the doctors,
the carpenters with wood?
There are bridges to be built,
and underprivileged to be understood.

Call out the peacemakers
armed with diplomacy and grit.
Silence those who wage foolish war
with contracted guards, and arguments unfit.

Paint the future, sketch a dream,
sing out in fervent praise!

For the end is nowhere close to us,
so do not countdown the days.

We enjoy the setting sun,
and provide lights to darkened skies
so dare not fear for us,
tomorrow with certainty, we again will arise.

Valuing Liberty
July 2007

Two hundred and thirty-one years ago John Adams suggested that all future Independence Day celebrations "ought to be solemnized with pomp and parade, with shows, games, sports, guns, bells, bonfires, and illuminations from one end of this continent to the other, from this time forward forevermore."

Celebrate we should, for in the successive generations since Adams, the nation and the world have dramatically changed; experiencing more freedom and a wider umbrella of democracy than ever before in the history of civilization. In doing so, however, we may have been losing some of the vital tenets of American liberty. Sometimes what we gain in experience we lose to arrogance. What we learn in technology we forget in compassion. Independence Day seems like a good time to reflect on our personal contributions to this grand experiment we so often take for granted. In modern America do we truly embrace the open debate of issues? Is the concept of "duty" revered as it once was? Is it the goal of every American to improve the nation?

Leader of the free world is a lofty self-proclaimed title for a relatively young nation. The character of the American citizen is unusual. We are brash, aggressive, driven, inventive, curious and passionate. But should we act as disciplinarian, the stern parent of a reckless world? I ask who better?

We are not a perfect people. No nation possesses perfection. Our form of government and its leaders, like our citizens, are flawed. We are a forgiving people, blessed with great compassion. Our history has earned us the role we play on this increasingly smaller planet. Although we have foibles, our founders and many of our leaders, the men and women we have put into the decision and influence making positions, whether through the ballot or through public interest, have sustained, tweaked, fiddled and continued to improve a very basic principle that has served humanity well. All men are created equal. Liberty and freedom bring out the best of people's minds and abilities. The consequence is that it can also bring out the worst, which is why such a high price is justly placed on values.

Values are intimate to each human being. However all citizens of a community must share some unifying values, whether that community be a family, a corporation, a nation or the world. The people of the United States of America value life, liberty and the pursuit of happiness. Our constitution is our guide. Like the Bible and many other great works, the contents are open to interpretation. America also values the right to debate, to criticize and to disagree. Many of our citizens have lived with our freedom for so long that even in the midst of war have taken it for granted, they forget, sadly, that much of the world does not have that luxury.

Until the entire world can appreciate freedom and is united in defeating oppressors of that inalienable human right, someone must stand up for it steadfast and consistently. Because we are the freest of nations we must defend all other nations and people pursuing liberation regardless of its tactical importance to our national security. For the biggest thereat to our national security is not color coded, it is the loss of liberty. That is why the words of John F. Kennedy still ring true today and should serve as a reminder until the world achieves peace.

"Let every nation know, whether it wishes us well or ill, that we shall pay any price, bear any burden, meet any hardship, support any friend, oppose any foe to assure the survival and the success of liberty."

If we do not believe those words today, we are not fully entitled to the freedom our predecessors fought so hard for.

Many have lost their appreciation for this great country and the people who add to its strength and character. It is not too late for each of us to contribute with our own elements of greatness. As true now as in past centuries, those with curiosity, tenacity, and optimism ought to be our celebrated heroes, regardless of their current role in our vast society.

Is Voting a Right, Privilege or Responsibility?

November 4, 2008

Is voting a right, privilege or responsibility? In the United States, if you are anything other than a middle-aged wealthy white landowner, it has been a hard fought right all too often taken for granted.

A license to drive a car is a privilege, not a right, and we're reminded that poor choices or circumstances can lead to your license being revoked. Sadly, there are those who ignore voting as a right and attempt to revoke it, to disenfranchise and suppress your voice and your power through misinformation, manipulation and even intimidation. Yes, voting is a fundamental right in this country; it is also a privilege.

When you vote, perhaps as a college student, a woman, a minority, or an immigrant here by choice, you are standing on the shoulders of those before you. Those who fought in our own streets and busses and courtrooms, and those who fought and continue to fight overseas to defend and protect the nation and its citizens, prop you up. The debt to be paid is the right and privilege of voting for issues that concern your community, state and nation. Voting for representatives, elected women and men who may or may not share your views but are open to debate and discourse.

During this time of year, I hear people talk while waiting in lines for their coffee or sandwiches, about the candidates or issues on the ballot. There are those who are meticulous in their research before forming an opinion of the issues versus those who will vote the party line, even if they need to block their nose while doing it. Those who ultimately vote based on who they would prefer to have a beer with could negate either of these choices. It is infuriating and beautifully American. We all have various amounts of influence in our lives – but in the voting booth, we are all equal and those who show up make the decisions.

There used to be a 'Liberty Mutual' advertisement on television that showed a determined wheelchair-bound voter face a series of obstacles. I often wonder at which point do people get deterred. What's your threshold? If it's raining, do you still go to the polls? If you are in a wheelchair, do you still go to the polls? If you must wait for a bus, do you still go to the polls? If the easily accessible entrance is blocked, do you find a way in? And there may be some additional obstacles this year. With misinformation on polling places and unscrupulous practices, have you educated yourself? With apathy, either, "We can't win," or "It's a shoe in," will you still vote? What about long lines? Two, four, five hours or more, will that discourage you? I believe this year, unlike years past, Americans are going to go and once again be heard. People know their vote is important. The 2000 Presidential election was separated by just 537 votes in Florida.

When new democracies emerge across the globe, it isn't uncommon to see long lines stretch into the streets as citizens get their first taste of freedom. Never before were they asked their opinion. Never before were they given the power to choose their future. In America, we have been blessedly spoiled. Granted, much of the population would prefer to vote from the comfort of their couch as if watching "American Idol" or "Dancing with the Stars" but something is different this year. Some of it is to participate in history, but more than that, it is to participate in a rebirth.

By now, few can argue that some things in the last four to eight years went terribly wrong. America, the 'Shinning City', has been badly tarnished and it's beacon obscured by fog. There was a time, as we searched for meaning and healing that American flags blanketed the nation and slogans of unity were draped over bridges. The sense of grit and determination was balanced with pride and love of country and of countrymen. It could have been our finest hour, but the goodwill was squandered.

Soon we witnessed the erosion of common sense and common decency. Victims became the accused. To question power became unpatriotic. Natural disasters begged for attention. We could almost hear the sobs of mourning come from our Constitution as we traded rights for false senses of security but lost some freedom, some privacy and as we debated the merits of torture. Some honor. We now are engaged in two brutal wars, which are aging too fast, and an economic turmoil that is likely in its infancy.

It is in this climate that America chooses a new leader (neither of whom was born in the continental United States). Americans want their country back. Be it for change, or for reform, the reason the electorate feels different this year is because in many ways the nation is going through a restoration. Challenges in the Middle East, the economy, energy, the environment, healthcare, education, social security and housing are ever present and not particularly new, but the approach we take to address each of them has to be.

We are at a defining moment; still deep in a dark forest, we must choose one of two paths. The certainty of either is unknown. One may lead in a circle; one may lead to a clearing. They may even run parallel. By now, we all have our preferences. The beauty of our system, our constitution and the very soul of the nation is that we are able to right our wrongs beginning on Election Day. Today the course will be set by the collective judgment of the American people. Your right, your privilege, your responsibility is to make absolutely sure your voice is heard.

Thoughts on Cheering Freedom

June 17, 2009

Whenever people stand up for a change against a repressive status quo, it invigorates me, be it an instant or a slow progression, it is still evolution. Even if the change they're seeking isn't substantively different. Any moment that arouses the hearts and minds of people to stand up, seek truth and take peaceful action is a moment deserving of applause and support. When any nation moves closer to democracy or its populace exert an effort to become "more perfect" it is cause for celebration. When citizens take action to expose its own nations' hypocrisy - all the better.

Perhaps this belief is a mix of nature and nurture that churns within me. My grandfather rescued his family and countless others in 1940's Europe by skillfully squeezing past the suffocating grip of Nazi Germany and the advancing Soviet Russia. I was born and raised in Massachusetts where details about the heroic efforts of patriots in the American Revolution were weaved into school trips and bicentennial celebrations. In college, I walked along the same Boston streets and stood alongside the shadows of the same historic buildings and landmarks that witnessed the forming of our nation.

While in college, I watched the televised protests in Tiananmen Square, the tearing down of the Berlin Wall, the fall of the Soviet Union and the liberation of former Iron Curtained states. And although this nation has seen its own travesties, it remains the beacon of hope, a model for young republics and the envy of freedom loving people.

In contrast to twenty years ago, the newspapers and cable news organizations of today are comparatively impotent, but the Internet, the greatest and most affordable conduit of ideas civilization has ever seen, has come alive. YouTube, Facebook, Flickr and most notably Twitter have provided instant images and perspective from participants, sympathizers, foes and opportunists alike. At times, feeds of information channels have adopted a mob mentality themselves as revolutions have become participative. Disinformation, panic, fear, lemming-like regurgitation of conflicting stories have been mixed together with bravery, images of compassion, and ever present hope. The naive and the knave, the instigators, the healers, the scholars and the rogues all compete for attention. It is frustratingly difficult to separate the signal from the noise. Yet, if you love the pursuit of freedom, it is also beautiful.

Margaret Mead said, "Never doubt that a small group of thoughtful, committed citizens can change the world. Indeed, it's the only thing that ever has." Still, cynics say there is no appreciable difference people sipping cappuccinos or playing on their Wii can have half a world away. That symbolic acts like tinting your profile picture green or other signs of solidarity are equivalent to giving an alcoholic vagrant a dollar. It makes you feel better, clears your soul, but doesn't address the core issue. Maybe. Maybe not. How can you know?

Freedom is addictive and any citizen of a free society enjoys seeing more of it. Realism tells us there is nothing we can individually do to affect change. However, realism didn't win the American Revolution. Faith, hope, determination and other intangibles did. So too, do those intangibles work today with every freedom loving movement.

Given our long history, freedom is a relatively new concept to humankind. It is still a fragile thing but it is desirable and we know we achieve greater things when we have it. Whether we broadcast it, or know it quietly in our heart, those who have a taste of freedom will always cheer and help those who are not. And in some incalculable way, make a difference in the process.

A Parent America

July 4, 2009

Like most Americans, I become exceptionally patriotic around July 4th and introspective about the nation's history, my own history, and the future of both. I vividly recall backyard barbecues, some of which were warm and delightful and some soggy but equally memorable. I remember our nation's bicentennial celebration and setting firecrackers off, much to my mother's dismay. I remember how firework shows terrified me as a child but now bring inspiration, awe and pride. I recall ad hoc barbecues in Boston and spending all day at the Esplanade waiting for the Boston Pops to perform. My wife and I celebrated our first Independence Day together as a married couple on the rooftop with friends. The night was full of music and synchronized colors. Soon the finale and all its illumination transformed the evening into daylight. The crackle and boom sounded like a war and we smiled with exhilaration and expectant joy.

Sadly, the nation has been through several real wars since then and undoubtedly, there will be more. Our nephews, cousins and friends have seen combat or have been stationed in some of the most dangerous places on earth. It occurred to me, and thankfully, he does not know it, since my son's birth in 2003, the nation has not been at peace. The resources of the country are so grand, the sacrifices of others so great that he has been insulated from the harsh realities of war.

I recently watched a report from an embedded journalist in Afghanistan who was caught up in a firefight. The action was loud and captured the attention and imagination of my curious boy. His questions on who was fighting and why, and if they were dying and why, became increasingly difficult to answer. I found myself explaining terrorism and how brave men and women protect us every day. That yes, some die and no, they do not get the same attention that Michael Jackson does and that's one reason why we should always thank those who volunteer to protect us.

How do we explain America to our children? That people wanting to do harm to us is not a new thing. That although we are peace loving, we are also a violent and brash culture? That for all our problems and dysfunction, like our insatiable consumption of drugs, our fascination with any salacious story, our self-inflicted pain caused by antiquated healthcare, education, and infrastructure systems, we are also envied? Why? Because the American gene pool is made up of leaders, innovators, artists, and visionaries. People from every nation in the world have risked their lives to come here, to worship, to love, to create something better.

At 233 years, we are a relatively young nation culturally, but our form of government is one of the more enduring compared to the 203 other nations on the planet. Yet, we are envied for the same reason we are hated. We value freedom and because we have it, we often take it for granted. We seem to treasure it most when it's at risk; otherwise, because we are fairly secure in it, something else often captures our attention.

Consider the television coverage of the conflict in Iran. The voices there hint at a fragile democracy, much like our forefathers did, though educated women, young and old, buoy this movement predominantly. It's a story that should transfix us. Freedom is on the march. Instead, it is put to the side in favor of a more accessible political sex scandal or Michael Jackson's premature death. We believe celebrity mystique is more appropriate summer fare than revolution. Revolutions seem to fit better in the autumn, after we've recharged our batteries but before the holidays. What hubris. What audacity. What truth. Detractors think it's blissful ignorance. That to be truly great, we need to organize our problems and solve them in a linear way. America doesn't work that way. This nation has the talent, enthusiasm, and skill to solve almost any problem. That's why it's so maddening when we don't address critical problems more timely. We could make things easier for ourselves, but as Americans, the easy way is seldom the most fun and we like a challenge.

What our nation has is boldness and maturity. Many nations are similar to the kids in the backseat of a car on a road trip. Sometimes we all sing or play fun games together, but invariably they ask, "Are we there yet?" They are vocal. They complain. They want us to pull over just as we are gathering speed. The one thing they never do is drive - nor do they want to. America is the parent. Our population's attitude follows a continuum between the reluctant parent and the kind who are smothering. Like a parent, we will often question our abilities, our decisions, and ourselves. Others will challenge our authority, rebel, ask for money and sometimes seek our hugs. It is not our role to whine about it. It is our role to lead it. The world expects that of us.

Enjoy your weekend and the parades, fireworks, and celebrations. Thank those who came before you quietly, and those who protect you loudly, and then dedicate yourself to finding your own special way of leading and making the nation and the world better in some way, grand or small.

they and me can again be We

They can gawk.
They can mock.
They can swear,
and blame,
and fail to understand.

They can fear.
They can demonize.
They can protect what they know.
They can try to keep their status quo,
with ignorance or denial.

They can rouse their forces,
weaponized beyond proportion.
They can spray the eyes or pull the hair
of mothers or daughters or elders,
who will no longer sit.
They can crack the heads of unarmed soldiers
who, for a decade risked their lives in far-off lands
to preserve the promise of days like these.

They can speak from two sides,
pretending they don't betray the constitution,
or morality, or commonsense.
They can tear down tents, disperse crowds
and destroy property of a free people.
They can invoke the cry of safety
to trump any law.

They can herd the young and old like cattle,
or throw men over barricades,
like worn-out mattresses.

They can disinfect parks sullied by occupation,
but not the hearts of an educated nation.

They can say they'll fix the wrongs.
They can bargain for more time,
in hopes bygones will be forgot.
They will not.

They can try to silence what's already been heard.
They can try to obfuscate what's already been seen.
They can try to blame the odor on others,
like children who hide the stink.
They can try to ignore the taste of justice
that brews in cafés and cafeterias and classrooms
and the places where debate is still safe and
welcome.
They can feel satisfied when streets are cleared
and they think things return to normal.
They can throw money at any problem,
because it is easier to find than good judgement.

They could find a cure in the sea of faces,
that hold the common man, woman and child,
doing uncommon things for the good of each other.

Then they, and me,
can again, be we.
And we, can overcome anything.

Never Be Frozen By Fear

I had a nightmare recently, the kind that makes you wake up in a cold sweat. This is rare for me as I have what I consider a gift, in that I found I have the ability to control my dreams. It started in early childhood when I was terrorized by Snuffalufagus and The Count from Sesame Street. They used to routinely chase me around a neighborhood grocery store and it was terrifying. I eventually trained myself to make them stop. I take this as a point of pride and it has often spared me uncomfortable dreams. If I don't like the direction one is going, my mind calls for a rewrite and I revise the plot. Not so the other night. I was completely frozen and could not control the outcome.

Who knows how the crazy world of dreams puts you in one predicament or another. In this one, I frightfully clung to a cliff. The sun was setting over the ocean, casting a deceptively peaceful golden light while the winds grew stronger.

Perhaps because of my training in television and film, I have found I am frequently able to control the angles or the "shots" of the movie in my mind. Like a director in the control room, I've been conscious of my ability to zoom in and out and to pan or dolly to get a better, more cinematic view of my surroundings. This nightmare was no exception, but doing so made my peril more visible. As I zoomed out it became clear that I was not clinging to a cliff, but a large rock formation beyond a cliff. Perhaps, I remember thinking; if I were able to scale it, I would be able to safely leap back to land. Unfortunately, as often happens in dreams, there were unexpected obstacles. The texture of this weathered rock was smooth with very few crevices to grasp. It also appeared that this rock disguised a marine geyser similar to La Buffadora in Mexico. It acted as a volcano and the top of it threatened to explode huge violent streams of water at any moment.

In my twenties, I participated in a ROPES program with a group of at-risk-kids. The day was filled with trust walks and physical and mental obstacle courses. One of the last challenges was to don a harness and scale a telephone pole, stand on top of it and leap toward a flag that was suspended slightly above it. The belayer controlling the rope from the ground would mitigate the fall. By that time in the day, I was physically exhausted and my legs had turned to jelly. I scaled the pole just fine, but I couldn't unlock my legs enough to stand. Ultimately, I decided to push myself off and I flailed toward the hanging flag. I missed it but remained safely cradled in the harness as I was unceremoniously lowered to the ground.

While stuck on this rock that memory engulfed me. Unfortunately, this was four times higher and there was no harness and nothing but waves and rocks below. I couldn't judge if I would be able to dive past the rocks into the ocean. The strengthening wind made me doubt it. I was paralyzed and felt a complete loss of control. Standing there, clinging to a rock, the wind battering me, with the threat of the unknown above me, and uncertainty below me.

Much of my nightmare was just the prolonged anguish of witnessing myself in that pose. It was a horrific feeling and I could no longer stand it. I continued to look upward and downward in utter indecisiveness. It was then I woke in that cold sweat. Awake and breathless, I replayed the scenario in my head. Why was this a nightmare?

The thought occurred to me; how many times do we have to face difficult choices armed with limited knowledge? The choice to move in one direction has uncertainty. A misstep or a random disruptive influence from the outside world could be catastrophic. The choice to move in the other direction may have a more definitive outcome, but it too is a lousy option.

In my dream, if I was able to climb up, I might have been visible to a rescue helicopter. Or, I might have been blown off the side. If I leapt off into the ocean below, it is likely I could have perished from the fall, if not the waves crashing against the rocks. Maybe I could have stayed and waited it out. Perhaps the tide would rise above the rocks. But then it would be night and I was already exhausted clinging for life. How much more could I endure?

That is what made it a nightmare. To have absolutely no control over the situation and to be paralyzed by fear and inaction. I morbidly began to think on where I would have most liked to have my body found. Clinging to a rock in fear, or somewhere else that showed I at least tried.

It may seem, at certain times in your life that you have no control over the situation you are in. This may be true, but you are always able to control how you respond to these situations. Huddle down, assess your options, and then take action. Sometimes, though rarely, waiting can be an appropriate action – if you've assessed your options and made that a conscious decision rather than a fall back to inaction.

Never be frozen by fear. You can never know the result of your decision ahead of time. It may be good or it may be bad, but you will certainly get immediate feedback once you've made it. Then, you will need to make another decision based on what you've learned. And then another and another. Make them. Make decisions and accept the consequences of them. Choose decisively and keep moving forward.

For the Love of Boston

April 17, 2013

I've been madly in love with Boston my entire life. In some ways, Patriot's Day is a celebration of our first date. Even though I'm in the opposite corner of the country, that love has never felt stronger than it has this week.

Patriot's Day is special in Massachusetts. When I was a child, I'd wear a tri-cornered hat, pull my socks up over my pant legs to mimic a minuteman, grab a toy rifle and hold my own reenactment in the backyard. My Dad brought me to Lexington Green, and Concord Bridge several times and it was always a special treat to go into town and visit the observation deck of the Pru, or the John Hancock, where they used to have an educational presentation on Boston's rich history. I remember tiny, white light bulbs on a huge map illuminated the route Paul Revere took on the evening of April 18, 1775. After the show, I would stare out the huge windows of the observation deck and take in the panoramic view of all the wondrous sites mentioned.

Coming from Boston, I have always felt pride in terms like 'patriot', 'minutemen' and 'the tea party', and it has always annoyed me when other groups around the nation co-opt those words to better market their political purpose, often sullying the name and cheapening the history in the process.

Patriot's Day has always been one of my favorite holidays. You didn't get presents, but you got out of school or work and into the spring air. One year we joined the masses at Hopkinton, to witness the start of the big race. For most of my youth, if we didn't watch on television, we'd fight traffic and find a place along Route 9, somewhere in the middle of the course. We'd stand on the roof of my dad's brown Dodge Dart and wait along with everyone else, to cheer for the runners. First came those in wheelchairs whom you admired for their determination. Then came the elite runners, whom you admired for their athleticism. Then, mixed among neighbors and friends, were local heroes and personalities. Workers from big companies ran together, engaged in a bonding exercise. Small teams and individuals ran for a cause, raising funds for cancer, or a fallen family member. The roar of the crowd for this wave of runners was deafening. The cheers helped motivate people ever forward. Volunteers held out Dixie cups of water and orange slices amidst shouts of encouragement and the ever-present unrelenting applause. You couldn't help but feel great after attending the Boston Marathon. By the time I was in college and beyond, I watched the final leg along Boylston Street, often a few feet from the finish line.

I'd often reminisce while walking the streets of Boston. When I was very young, and still in the suburbs, my mother and grandmother used to drag me on to a train to "go to the city" and shop at places like Jordan Marsh and Filene's and I'm sure we had lunch at Woolworths. I'd be pulled along the cobblestone sidewalks of the Freedom Trail without complaint. We'd visit the Granary Burial ground, the final resting place of many early patriots, including my favorite, Paul Revere.

On other occasions, my older brothers and sister could always be counted on to score a few seats in Fenway at least a couple of times each season, when Lynn, Rice and Evans where in the outfield.

Although I visited many campuses in New England, when it came time for college, there was never any real doubt I would go someplace in Boston. I chose Emerson, where I lost my accent and found my voice. It's where I grew up. Boston is where I met my best friends, had my first real kiss, learned how to lead, and how to write. Boston is where I fell in love. I proposed to my wife on the bridge in the Public Garden. We wed in the Copley Plaza Hotel, a block away from where the marathon finished. We lived in a small apartment above an art gallery on Newbury Street, a block away from the finish line in the other direction.

At that time in my life, I fully realized feeling of Boston being the 'Hub of the Universe.' It was the hub of my universe, particularly Back Bay.

I moved to California twenty years ago, but a big part of me never really left Boston. My wife and my young family would make it a point to visit my parents in the suburbs, and eventually down the Cape, whenever possible, but the trip wasn't complete until we spent some time in the city.

Whenever a business trip brought me back East, I would nearly always finagle a side trip to Boston, even if just for a few hours.

I find it hard to describe the spirit of Boston to those who have never been. The city has an intimacy of scale, but an enormous vitality. Yes, there is arrogance, usually justified. Yes, there is belligerence, usually not justified. And, particularly refreshing after spending time on the West coast, there is brutal honesty and raucous humor. If you want warm memories in your life, spend a cold day in Boston. Last year my father and I went in for the day. The cosmopolitan energy was immediate. It refueled me. Once touched, you feel like you'll never run on empty again.

I've learned that others who've spent formative years in Boston, and we're everywhere, have all had similar experiences. This realization is not met with scarcity or jealousy over someone riding the coattails of your memory. Instead, there is an immediate palpable bond and kinship. Once you're a Bostonian, you're always a Bostonian.

Every time I see images of Boston, my heart flutters and I get giddy, like seeing an old crush. To see the horrific images coming out of Boston this week were heartbreaking, not only because of the carnage and the attack on the very spirit of the day, but also, and I know I'm not alone in this, because it felt extremely personal. The sidewalks soaked in the blood of innocent people are sidewalks I've travelled thousands of times. The pictures shown were of my old turf, my backyard, my front yard, and my living room. Those places were the inspiration and settings for my books and indeed my life in general. To see those sidewalks, my sidewalks, engulfed in destruction causes a pain that cuts in ways I struggle to articulate.

When organizations and individuals make declarations that this cataclysm changes the city, and the marathon forever, it simultaneously saddens and angers me. They misunderstand the spirit of the city and the resolve of Bostonians. Boston is the birthplace of the American Revolution. The city knows change, but it's change that comes on our terms, not because of an act of terror, hate and a cowardly pitiful cry for attention from the forces of evil. This traumatic event does not undermine our values it strengthens them. Yes, evil is present, but it didn't win. Witness the scores of people who instantaneously and heroically ran toward the blast, concerned only with helping others. Every time that happens, humanity wins. Bostonians in particular, do not cower or cave. Ever.

Perpetrators of evil will never win. There's no other way to say it. You can never, ever, fuck with Boston and expect to win. You will lose, and in time, Bostonians around the world, with sheer grit, will ultimately render you an irrelevant asterisk in the chronicle of our long history, enduring spirit and devotion to freedom and liberty. Boston is a gorgeous city and she's never looked finer.

Six Words of Advice for Writers

The written word can convey or challenge an idea and persuade action. That's what makes writing is a valuable leadership skill. Newspapers and traditional books sales may be down, but writing is up. Think about it. Anything you read, anything, was first written. Emails, reports, newsletters, reviews, eBooks, status updates on LinkedIn, Facebook or Twitter. What you see on television, in movies and at plays began at a written script to convey an idea. Yes, even "reality" shows.

If you want to work on your leadership, work on your writing. Here are six words of advice.

Write - Writers write. You have to face the blank page or screen and begin to fill it. Start with something; an outline, note cards, a napkin, it doesn't matter. Just begin.

Revise - No matter how eloquent you think you are, your first draft is bound to have a bit of uncertainty or a lack of clarity. It's rare to get it right on the very first pass. Rewriting makes things better. Cut, reword and simplify what you're trying to convey. Your readers will appreciate it.

Release - Eventually, you must stop your editing and revisions. At some point, while you were writing with a burst of inspiration you may have felt your work was genius; but now you're holding it back in an effort to make it perfect. This is a mistake. Most won't notice or care, and those that do, will always find something to criticize you on anyway. Let it go. It's time to share what you write with others.

Receive - Receive feedback on your work gracefully. Some will disagree with you, or be hypercritical. Some won't notice your words at all, but will be inexplicably moved by them. Be open and gracious. The author may never know how directly, but the written word always makes a difference.

Rejoice - Writing is about creating. Forming words in the right order to illicit a desired response and actually committing them to the page is no simple task. Sharing those idea and thoughts with others can expose vulnerabilities. That exposure is what keeps many from writing, and those who do write from becoming better. Writing is not an effortless activity so make the time to celebrate your achievement with everything you write. On occasion you may fail to articulate what you intended adequately. Celebrate anyway. You've demonstrated leadership in caring enough to capture your thoughts for the benefit of others.

Repeat - Do it again. Continue to hone the craft of writing. Laziness in writing is laziness in leadership so keep exercising. Even if you only write 140 characters at a time, make them sing. Just as in leadership, effective writing must mix art and science. Through repetition, you will begin to explore the nuances of each.

About the Author

Karl Bimshas, Boston-bred and California-chilled leadership consultant and author of several books and programs designed for busy professionals who want to manage better and lead well.

With an M.S. in Executive Leadership from the University of San Diego and a B.A. in Mass Communications from Emerson College in Boston, Karl Bimshas has held operational and sales leadership positions in public and private corporations. As a sought-after executive coach and leadership consultant, he's helped busy professionals find, set and get their great goals by discovering the a-ha within.

For more information, visit
www.KarlBimshasConsulting.com
or call 619-497-2670

www.ingramcontent.com/pod-product-compliance
Lightning Source LLC
Chambersburg PA
CBHW071036240526
45469CB00006BD/2229